CROCHET
Purse Panache!™

General Information

Many of the products used in this pattern book can be purchased from local craft, fabric and variety stores or from the Annie's Attic Needlecraft Catalog *(see Customer Service information on page 12)*.

Contents

Simply Suede Set	2
Cotton Trio	4
Stained Glass Orchid	6
Felted Fireworks	8
Midnight Magic	9
Pretty in Purple	10
Stitch Guide	11

Simply Suede Set

Designs by Kathleen Sams for Coats & Clark

Square Diagram

[Square diagram showing holes around the perimeter]

SHOULDER STRAP PURSE
SKILL LEVEL

EASY

FINISHED SIZE
5 inches square, not including strap

MATERIALS
- J. & P. Coats Speed-Cro-Sheen Size 3 fine (sport) weight crochet thread:
  100 yds. #61 new ecru
- Size F/5/3.75mm crochet hook or size needed to obtain gauge
- Tapestry needle
- Large brown suede trim piece
- Size 5 hole puncher

GAUGE
7 sc = 1½ inches; 3 sc rows = ½ inch

NOTE
Cut four 4-inch squares from suede. Using hole puncher, punch holes ¼ inch from outer edge, ½ inch apart (see diagram) on each piece.

INSTRUCTIONS
PURSE
Square No. 1
Rnd 1 (RS): With RS of one suede piece facing, join with sl st in any corner hole, *(2 sc, ch 2, 2 sc) in same hole, 2 sc in each of next 6 holes; rep from * around, join with sl st in first sc. *(64 sc made)*

Row 2: Now working in rows, sl st in next st, (sl st, ch 1, 2 sc) in corner ch sp, [sc in each of next 16 sc, 5 sc in corner ch-2 sp] 2 times, sc in each of next 16 sc, 2 sc in next ch-2 sp, turn leaving rem edge unworked for top edge.

Rows 3–6: Ch 1, sc in each sc across, turn. At end of last row, fasten off.

Square No. 2 (make 3)
Rnd 1: With RS of suede piece facing, join with sl st in any corner hole, *(2 sc, ch 2, 2 sc) in same hole, 2 sc in each of next 6 holes, rep from * around, join with sl st in first sc. *(64 sc made)*

Row 2: Now working in rows, sl st in next st, (sl st, ch 1, 2 sc) in corner ch sp, [sc in each of next 16 sc, 5 sc in corner ch-2 sp] 2 times, sc in each of next 16 sc, 2 sc in next ch-2 sp, turn leaving rem edge unworked for top edge. Fasten off.

Pocket
Row 1: Holding two Square No. 2's RS tog, working through both thicknesses, join with sl st in first st, sl st in each st across, turn leaving top edge unworked.

Rows 2–4: Ch 1, sc in each sc across, turn. At end of last row, fasten off.

FINISHING
1: Sew Pocket Squares *(front)* and Square No. 1 *(back)* tog across three edges leaving top edge unsewn.

2: Sew one side of last Square No. 2, to top edge of Square No. 1 for flap.

3: For **trim**, working around edges of flap and top edge on front, join with sc at side seam, evenly sp sc around, join with sl st in first sc. Fasten off.

4: For **strap**, ch 201, sl st in second ch from hook and in each ch across. Fasten off. Lace one end of strap through one side seam, tie in knot. Rep on other side with rem end.

PURSELET
SKILL LEVEL

EASY

FINISHED SIZE
3 inches square, not including strap

MATERIALS
- J. & P. Coats Speed-Cro-Sheen size 3 fine (sport) weight crochet thread:
  100 yds #61 new ecru
- Size F/5/3.75mm crochet hook or size needed to obtain gauge
- Tapestry needle
- Large brown suede trim piece
- Large wooden bead
- Size 5 hole puncher

GAUGE
7 sc = 1½ inches; 3 sc rows = ½ inch

NOTE
Cut two 2-inch squares from suede. Using hole puncher, punch holes ¼ inch from outer edge, ½ inch apart *(see diagram)* on each piece.

INSTRUCTIONS
PURSELET
Square (make 2)
Rnd 1: With RS of suede piece facing, join with sl st in any corner hole, 3 sc in same hole, [2 sc in each of next 2 holes, 3 sc in hole at corner] 3 times, 2 sc in each of last 2 holes, join with sl st in first sc. *(28 sc made)*
Rnd 2: Working in **back lps** *(see Stitch Guide)*, ch 1, sc in first st, [3 sc in next st, sc in each of next 6 sts] 3 times, 3 sc in next st, sc in each st around, join.
Rnd 3: Ch 1, sc in each st around with (sc, ch 2, sc) in each center corner st, join. Fasten off.

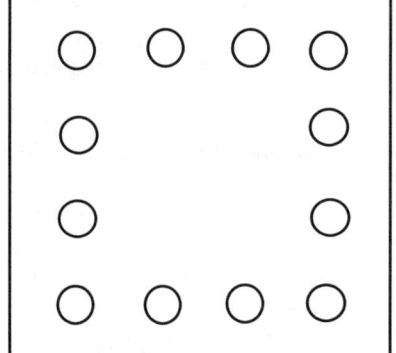
Square Diagram

Edging
Row 1: With RS of pieces tog, working through both thicknesses, join with sl st in corner ch sp, sl st in each st and ch sp around three edges leaving one edge open for top edge, turn.
Rnd 2: Turn piece RS out, working around top edge only, ch 1, sc in each st around, join with sl st in first sc.
Rnd 3: Ch 1, sc in each of first 6 sts, (sc, ch 10, sc) in next st *(button loop made)*, sc in each st around, join. Fasten off.
For **strap**, ch 155, sl st in second ch from hook and in each ch across. Fasten off.
Sew ends of strap to sides of Purselet.
Sew bead opposite button loop.❑❑

Cotton Trio

Designs by Glenda Winkleman for Coats & Clark

TRENDY CLUTCH

SKILL LEVEL

BEGINNER

FINISHED SIZE
8 inches wide x 6 inches high

MATERIALS
- Coats & Clark Speed-Cro-Sheen size 3 fine (sport) weight cotton thread: 200 yds #4 blue
- Size F/5/3.75mm crochet hook or size needed to obtain gauge
- Tapestry needle
- 1¼-inch wooden button

GAUGE
17 sc = 4 inches; 11 sc rows = 2 inches

INSTRUCTIONS
HANDBAG
Rnd 1: Ch 35, sc in second ch from hook and in each ch across with 3 sc in last ch, working on opposite side of ch, sc in each ch across with 2 sc in last ch, join with sl st in first sc. *(70 sc made)*

Rnd 2: Ch 1, 2 sc in first st, sc in each of next 32 sts, 2 sc in each of next 3 sts, sc in each st across to last 2 sts, 2 sc in each of last 2 sts, join. *(76)*

Rnds 3–32: Ch 1, sc in each st around, **do not join**. Mark first st of each rnd.

Row 33: Now working in rows for flap, sc in each first 38 sts, turn leaving rem sts unworked. *(38 sc)*

Row 34: Ch 1, sc in each st across, turn.

Row 35: Ch 1, **sc dec** *(see Stitch Guide)* in first 2 sts, sc in each st across to last 2 sts, sc dec in last 2 sts, turn. *(36)*

Rows 36–46: Ch 1, sc in each st across, turn.

Row 47: Ch 1, (sc, ch 2, sc) in first st, *sk next st, (sc, ch 2, sc) in next st; rep from * 7 times, ch 5 *(button loop)*, sk next 2 sts, (sc, ch 2, sc) in next st, [sk next st, (sc, ch 2, sc) in next st] across. Fasten off.

For **shoulder strap**, ch 200, (sc, ch 2, sc) in second ch from hook, [sk next ch, (sc, ch 2, sc) in next ch] across, ch 2, working on opposite side of ch, *(sc, ch 2, sc) in next ch, sk next ch; rep from * across, ch 2, join with sl st in first sc. Fasten off.

Sew 2 inches of ends on strap to outsides of Bag as shown in photo.

Sew button to Bag opposite button loop on flap.

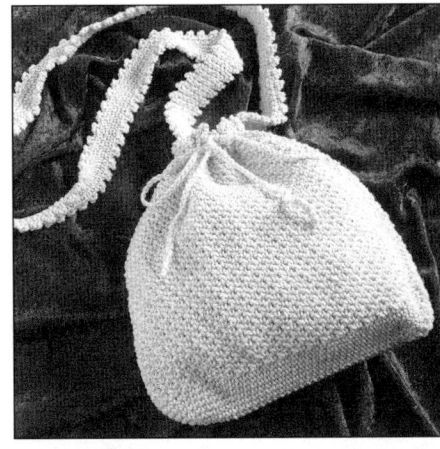

GRAB-IT HANDBAG

SKILL LEVEL

EASY

FINISHED SIZE
9¾ inches wide x 9 inches high

MATERIALS
- Coats & Clark Speed-Cro-Sheen size 3 fine (sport) weight cotton thread: 200 yds #61 new ecru
- Size F/5/3.75mm crochet hook or size needed to obtain gauge
- Tapestry needle

GAUGE
9 sc = 2¾ inches; 7 sc rows = 1½ inches

INSTRUCTIIONS
HANDBAG
Rnd 1: Ch 31, sc in second ch from hook and in each ch across with 4 sc in last ch; working on opposite side of ch, sc in each ch across with 3 sc in last ch, join with sl st in first sc. *(64 sc made)*

Rnd 2: Ch 1, 2 sc in first st, sc in each of next 28 sts, 2 sc in each of next 4 sts, sc in each of next 28 sts, 2 sc in each of last 3 sts, join. *(72)*

Rnd 3: Ch 1, 2 sc in each of first 2 sts, sc in each of next 28 sts, 2 sc in each of next 8 sts, sc in each of next 28 sts, 2 sc in each of last 6 sts, join. *(88)*

Rnds 4–7: Ch 1, sc in each st around, join.

Rnd 8: Ch 1, sc in first st, [dc in next st, sc in next st] around to last st, (dc, sc) in last st, **do not join**. Mark first st of each rnd.

Rnds 9–38: [Dc in each sc, sc in each dc] around.

Rnd 39: Sc in each st around, join with sl st in first sc.

Rnd 40: Sl st in next st, ch 4 *(counts as first dc and ch-1)*, sk next st, [dc in next st, ch 1, sk next st] around to last st, dc in last st, ch 1, join with sl st in third ch of ch-4.

Rnd 41: Ch 1, sc in each st and in each ch sp around, join.

Rnd 42: Ch 1, sc in each of first 2 sts, (ch 3, sl st) in top of last st made, [sc in each of next 2 sts, (ch 3, sl st) in top of last st made] around, join. Fasten off.

For **drawstring**, ch 160. Fasten off. Weave though ch sps on rnd 40. Tie knot in each end of drawstring.

Shoulder Strap

Rnd 1: Ch 190, sc in second ch from hook and in each ch across to last ch, 4 sc in last ch, working on opposite side of ch, sc in each ch around to last ch, 3 sc in last ch, join with sl st in first sc.

Rnd 2: Ch 1, sc in each of first 2 sts, (ch 3, sl st) in top of last st made, [sc in each of next 2 sts, (ch 3, sl st) in top of last st made] around, join. Fasten off.

Sew 1½ inch of each end to inside on each side of Bag.

MINI-DRAWSTRING

SKILL LEVEL

INTERMEDIATE

FINISHED SIZE

6½ inches high

MATERIALS
- ❑ Coats & Clark Speed-Cro-Sheen size 3 fine (sport) weight cotton thread: 200 yds #46A mid rose
- ❑ Size F/5/3.75mm crochet hook or size needed to obtain gauge

GAUGE

5 sts = 1 inch

INSTRUCTIONS

HANDBAG

Rnd 1: Ch 4, 11 dc in fourth ch from hook, join with sl st in top of ch-3. *(12 dc made)*

Rnd 2: Ch 1, 2 sc in first st, sc in next st, [2 sc in next st, sc in next st] around, join with sl st in first sc. *(18 sc)*

Rnd 3: Ch 3, dc in same st, 2 dc in each st around, join. *(36)*

Rnd 4: Ch 1, 2 sc in first st, sc in each of next 3 sts, [2 sc in next st, sc in each of next 3 sts] around, join. *(45)*

Rnd 5: Ch 3, dc in same st, dc in each of next 2 sts, [2 dc in next st, dc in each of next 2 sts] around, join. *(60)*

Rnd 6: Ch 1, sc in each st around, join.

Rnd 7: Ch 3, dc in each st around, join.

Rnd 8: Ch 1, sc in each st around, join.

Rnd 9: (Ch 1, sc, ch 2, sc) in first st, sk next st, *(sc, ch 2, sc) in next st, sk next st; rep from * around, **do not join rnds.** Mark first st of each rnd. *(30 ch-2 sps)*

Rnds 10–31: (Sc, ch 2, sc) in each ch-2 sp around.

Rnd 32: (Sc, ch 2, sc) in first ch-2 sp, sk next ch-2 sp, *(sc, ch 2, sc) in each of next 5 ch-2 sps, sk next ch-2 sp; rep from * around to last 4 ch-2 sps, (sc, ch 2, sc) in each of last 4 ch-2 sps. *(25 ch-2 sps)*

Rnd 33: 2 sc in each ch sp around, join with sl st in first sc. *(50 sc)*

Rnd 34: Ch 4 *(counts as first dc and ch-1)*, (dc, ch 1) in each st around, join with sl st in third ch of beg ch-4.

Rnd 35: Ch 1, (sc, ch 2, sc) in first ch sp, sk next ch sp, *(sc, ch 2, sc) in next ch sp, sk next ch sp; rep from * around, join. Fasten off.

For **drawstring,** ch 120. Fasten off. Weave drawstring through ch-1 sps of rnd 34.

For **shoulder strap,** ch 200, insert hook in ch-2 sp of rnd 35 in center at side of Handbag, insert hook in first ch of ch-200, yo, pull through all thicknesses, yo, pull through all lps on hook. Fasten off.

Rep shoulder strap on other side of Handbag.❑❑

Stained Glass Orchid

Design by Julia Bryant

SKILL LEVEL

INTERMEDIATE

FINISHED SIZE
9 inches wide x 8 inches high

MATERIALS
- Fine (sport) weight yarn:
    1¾ oz/175 yds/50g black
    1¾ oz/175 yds/50g lavender
    ½ oz/50 yds/14g green
    ½ oz/50 yds/14g dk pink
    ½ oz/50 yds/14g purple
- Size E/4/3.5mm crochet hook
- Size G/6/4mm afghan crochet hook or size needed to obtain gauge
- Tapestry needle
- ½ x 18-inch piece of plastic canvas

GAUGE
G hook: 5 sts = 1 inch; 5 rows = 1 inch

SPECIAL STITCH
For **color change,** drop current color, insert hook under next vertical bar, yo with new color, pull lp through, to work lps off hook, [work lps off until one lp of current color remains on hook, drop current color and pick up next color from under first color, yo, pull through 2 lps on hook] across.

Afghan Stitch Color Change
1: Drop last color to wrong side of work; pull up next lp with next color.

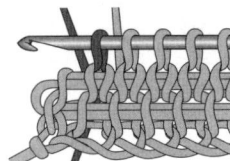

2: Drop last color to wrong side of work; work off next st with next color.

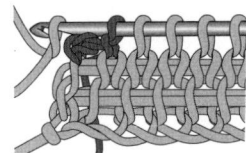

Do not carry yarn across back of work for more than two or three sts, use separate ball of yarn for each section of color, always pick up next color from under current color to prevent a gap from forming.

INSTRUCTIONS
PURSE
Back
Row 1: With afghan hook and lavender, ch 45, insert hook in second ch from hook, yo, pull up lp, pull up lp in each ch across leaving all lps on hook; to work

Afghan Stitch

a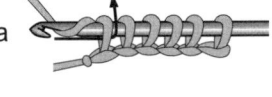

b

c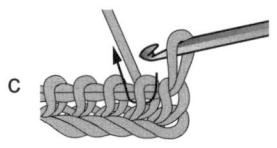

d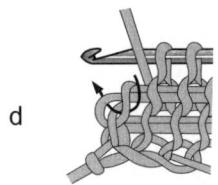

lps off hook, yo, pull though one lp on hook *(see illustration a)*, [yo, pull through 2 lps on hook] across *(see illustration b)* leaving last lp on hook at end of each row, **do not turn.** Last lp on hook is first st of next row.

Row 2: Sk first vertical bar, for **afghan st**, [insert hook under next vertical bar *(see illustration c),* yo, pull up lp] across to last vertical bar leaving all lps on hook; for **last st,** insert hook under last bar and st directly behind it *(see illustration d)*, yo, pull lp through bar and st; work lps off hook.

Rows 3–38: Sk first vertical bar, afghan st across; work lps off hook.

Row 39: To bind off, sl st in each vertical bar across. Fasten off.

Front
Row 1: With afghan hook and black, ch 45, pick up lp in second ch from hook and in each ch across; work lps off hook.

Rows 2–38: Work in afghan st across, changing colors *(see Special Stitch)* according to graph; work lps off hook.

Row 39: To bind off, sl st in each vertical bar across. Fasten off.

Top Facing
Row 1: With RS of Back facing and crochet hook, working in **back lps** *(see Stitch Guide)*, join black with sl st in first st, ch 3 *(counts as first dc)*, dc in each st across, turn. *(45 dc made)*

Rows 2 & 3: Ch 3, dc in each st across, turn. At end of last row, fasten off.

Rep across top edge of Front.

Cut two pieces of plastic canvas to fit across top edge.

Turn facing to the inside on each piece and sew in place covering one piece of plastic canvas.

With WS of Front and Back tog, working through all thicknesses, with crochet hook and black, sc tog across sides and bottom. Fasten off.

For **handle,** cut 12 strands black each 68 inches in length. Divide into three groups of four stands each. Braid groups tog leaving 4 inch ends for tassel. Tie knot in each end and trim even.

Sew ends of handle above tassel to sides of Purse as shown in photo.❑❑

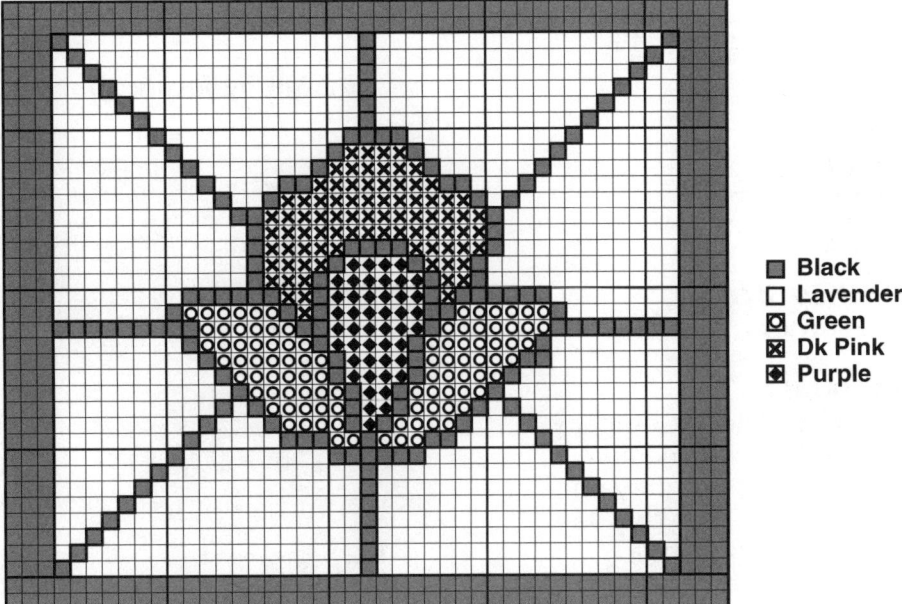

Stained Glass Orchid Graph

■ Black
☐ Lavender
◙ Green
☒ Dk Pink
✦ Purple

Felted Fireworks

Design by Jackie Young

SKILL LEVEL

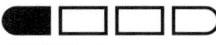

BEGINNER

FINISHED SIZE
6 x 9 inches

MATERIALS
- Brown Sheep Company Lamb's Pride medium (worsted) weight yarn: 3¾ oz/190 yds/106g #M-23 fuchsia
- Trendsetter Shadow or fine (sport) weight eyelash yarn: .7 oz/73 yds/20g #1 black multi
- Size N crochet hook
- Tapestry needle
- 1-inch button

NOTE
The size before felting will be about 7½ x 10 inches. Don't worry too much about gauge; strive for a loose, open look in your stitches.

INSTRUCTIONS

HANDBAG

Rnd 1: With fuchsia, ch 21, sc in second ch from hook and in each ch across with 3 sc in last ch; working on opposite side of ch, sc in each ch across with 2 sc in last ch, **do not turn or join rnds.** *(42 sc made)*

Next Rnds: Sc in each st around until piece measures 8 inches from beg.

Next Rnd: Holding eyelash and fuchsia yarn tog as one, sc in each st around.

Next Rnds: Rep last rnd until piece measures 10 inches from beg.

Next Rnd: Sc in first 21 sts, ch 10 *(button loop)*, sc in each st around.

For **strap**, make ch 42 inches in length, sl st in opposite side of Handbag, **turn**, sc in each ch across, sl st in same st as first ch. Fasten off.

To **felt bag**, using hottest water and the smallest size load, felt the bag in the washing machine. Run through two 10-minute cycles or until bag is felted to your liking. Pull into shape and lay flat to dry.

Sew button opposite button loop.

Midnight Magic

Design by Jackie Young

SKILL LEVEL

EASY

FINISHED SIZE
7 x 10 inches

MATERIALS
- Cascade 220 wool (medium) worsted yarn (220 yds/100g per hank):
  1 hank #8555 black
- Funny eyelash (light) weight novelty yarn (99 yds/50g per ball):
  2 balls #1080 black/gold
- Size N crochet hook
- Tapestry needle
- Special pin or large sparkly button

NOTE
The size before felting will be about 8 x 12 inches. Don't worry too much about gauge; strive for a loose open look in your stitches.

INSTRUCTIONS
HANDBAG
Rnd 1: With one strand of each yarn held tog, ch 25, sc in sec-

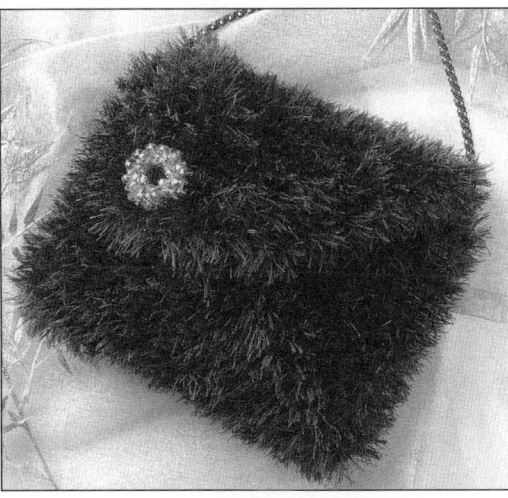

ond ch from hook and in each ch across with 3 sc in last ch; working on opposite side of ch, sc in each ch across with 2 sc in last ch, **do not turn or join,** mark first st of each rnd. *(50 sc made)*

Rnd 2: Sc in each st around.

Next Rnds: Rep rnd 2 until piece measures 8 inches from beg, ending at side edge.

Next Row: Now working in rows for **flap**, sc in first 24 sts, turn leaving rem sts unworked. *(24 sc)*

Next Row: Ch 1, sk first st, sc in each of next 23 sts, turn. *(23)*

Next Row: Ch 1, sc in each st across, turn.

Next Rows: Rep last row until flap measures 3 inches, ending with RS row.

Next Row: Ch 1, **sc dec** *(see Stitch Guide)* in first 2 sts, sc in each st across, turn. *(22)*

Next Row: Ch 1, sc in each st across to last 2 sts, sc dec in last 2 sts, turn. *(21)*

Next Rows: Rep last 2 rows alternately until you have 12 sts rem, ending with RS row.

Next Row: Ch 1, sc dec in next 2 sts, sc in each of next 3 sts, ch 3 *(button loop),* sk next 3 sts, sc in each of last 4 sts, turn.

Next Row: Ch 1, sc in each of first 4 sts, sc in each of next 3 chs, sc in each of next 2 sts, sc dec in last 2 sts, turn.

Last Row: Ch 1, sc in each st across. Fasten off.

To **felt bag,** using hottest water and the smallest size load, felt the bag in the washing machine. Run through two 10-minute cycles or until bag is felted to your liking. Pull into shape and lay flat to dry.

Sew button or pin on pin opposite button loop.

Pretty in Purple

Design by Jenny King

SKILL LEVEL
INTERMEDIATE

FINISHED SIZE
11 x 18½ inches including handles

MATERIALS
- Brown Sheep Company Cotton Fleece medium (worsted) weight yarn:
    3½ oz/215 yds/99g purple
    3½ oz/215 yds/99g lavender
    3½ oz/215 yds/99g white
- Sizes G/6/4mm and H/8/5mm crochet hooks or size needed to obtain gauge
- Tapestry needle

GAUGE
G hook: 5 sc = 1 inch; 4 rows = 1 inch

INSTRUCTIONS

BAG
Side (make 1 purple and 1 lavender)

Row 1: With G hook, ch 20, sc in second ch from hook and in each ch across with 3 sc in last ch; working on opposite side of ch, sc in each ch across, turn. *(39 sc made)*

Rows 2–20: Ch 1, sc in each st across, turn.

Row 21: Ch 1, sk first st, sc in each st across to last st, turn leaving last st unworked. *(37)*

Rows 22–24: Ch 1, sc in each st across, turn.

Rows 25–65: Rep rows 21–24 consecutively, ending with row 21 and 15 sts.

Rows 66–83: Ch 1, sc in each st across, turn. At end of last row, fasten off.

Center Panel
Row 1: With G hook and white, ch 21; sc in second ch from hook and in each ch across, turn. *(20 sc made)*

Rows 2–88: Ch 1, sc in each st across, turn. At end of last row, fasten off.

Using lavender for the purple Side and purple for the lavender Side, sc Center to each Side as shown in photo. Fasten off.

For **trim,** with white, sl st ends of Side pieces tog at top to form handle; working in ends of rows around opening, evenly sl st around; working back across first sts, sl st in each st across, evenly sl st around opening, join with sl st in first sl st on this opening. Fasten off.

The flower is made using two strands of yarn held tog as one and in one long continuous strand. The petals are then arranged one on top of the other to create the 3-D effect. Change the flower color by changing a new color at the ch-4 *(see illustration)*, leaving a 4 inch end of each color. Twist or braid all the ends tog and place between the flower and the Bag to add padding when complete.

Color Change in Chain

For **flower,** with two strands of yarn and H hook, ch 2, *(sc, ch 3) 5 times in second ch from hook, sl st in same ch *(5 petals made)***, ch 4 *(change one or more colors)*; rep from * 3 times, ending last rep at **. Leaving a 12 end for sewing, fasten off.

Arrange and sew flower to Center as shown or as desired.

StitchGuide.com

STANDARD ABBREVIATIONS

beg	beginning
ch, chs	chain, chains
dc	double crochet
dec	decrease
hdc	half double crochet
inc	increase
lp, lps	loop, loops
rnd, rnds	round, rounds
sc	single crochet
sl st	slip stitch
sp, sps	space, spaces
st, sts	stitch, stitches
tog	together
tr	treble crochet
yo	yarn over

Single crochet decrease (sc dec): (Insert hook, yo, draw up a lp) in each of the sts indicated, yo, draw through all lps on hook.

Half double drochet decrease (hdc dec): (Yo, insert hook, yo, draw lp through) in each of the sts indicated, yo, draw through all lps on hook.

Double crochet decrease (dc dec): (Yo, insert hook, yo, draw lp through, yo, draw through 2 lps on hook) in each of the sts indicated, yo, draw through all lps on hook.

Front post stitch—fp: Back post stitch—bp: When working post st, insert hook from right to left around post of st on previous row.

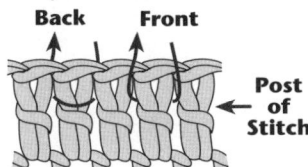

Chain—ch: Yo, pull through lp on hook.

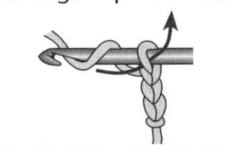

Slip stitch—sl st: Insert hook in st, yo, pull through both lps on hook.

Single crochet—sc: Insert hook in st, yo, pull through st, yo, pull through both lps on hook.

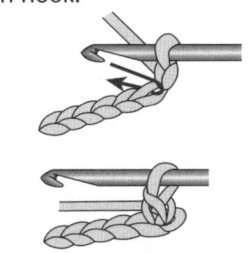

Front loop—front lp: Back loop—back lp:

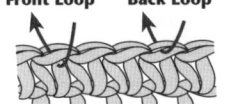

Change colors: Drop first color; with second color, pull through last 2 lps of st.

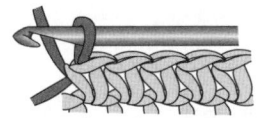

Half double crochet—hdc: Yo, insert hook in st, yo, pull through st, yo, pull through all 3 lps on hook.

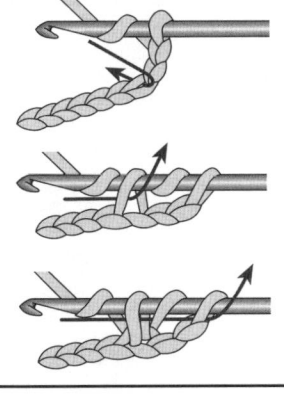

Double crochet—dc: Yo, insert hook in st, yo, pull through st, (yo, pull through 2 lps) 2 times.

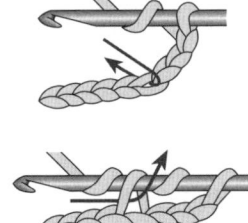
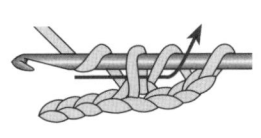
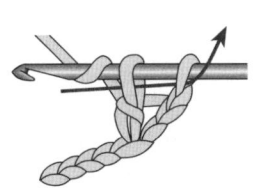

Treble crochet—tr: Yo 2 times, insert hook in st, yo, pull through st, (yo, pull through 2 lps) 3 times.

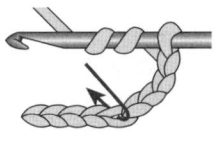
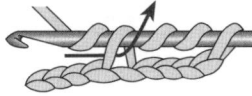

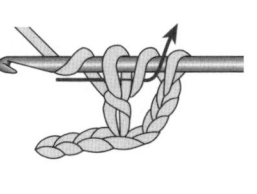
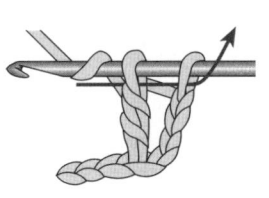

Double treble crochet—dtr: Yo 3 times, insert hook in st, (yo, pull through 2 lps) 4 times.

The patterns in this book are written using American crochet stitch terminology. For our international customers, hook sizes, stitches and yarn definitions should be converted as follows: *But, as with all patterns, test your gauge (tension) to be sure.*

US	UK
sl st (slip stitch)	= sc (single crochet)
sc (single crochet)	= dc (double crochet)
hdc (half double crochet)	= htr (half treble crochet)
dc (double crochet)	= tr (treble crochet)
tr (treble crochet)	= dtr (double treble crochet)
dtr (double treble crochet)	= ttr (triple treble crochet)
skip	= miss

THREAD/YARNS

Bedspread Weight	=	No. 10 Cotton or Virtuoso
Sport Weight	=	4 Ply or thin DK
Worsted Weight	=	Thick DK or Aran

MEASUREMENTS

1 inch	=	2.54 cm
1 yd.	=	.9144 m
1 oz.	=	28.35 g

CROCHET HOOKS

Metric	US	Metric	US
.60mm	14	3.00mm	D/3
.75mm	12	3.50mm	E/4
1.00mm	10	4.00mm	F/5
1.50mm	6	4.50mm	G/6
1.75mm	5	5.00mm	H/8
2.00mm	B/1	5.50mm	I/9
2.50mm	C/2	6.00mm	J/10

306 East Parr Road
Berne, IN 46711
© 2004 Annie's Attic

TOLL-FREE ORDER LINE or to request a free catalog (800) LV-ANNIE (800) 582-6643
Customer Service (800) AT-ANNIE (800) 282-6643, **Fax** (800) 882-6643
Visit www.AnniesAttic.com
We have made every effort to ensure the accuracy and completeness of these instructions.
We cannot, however, be responsible for human error, typographical mistakes or variations in individual work.
Reprinting or duplicating the information, photographs or graphics in this publication by any means,
including copy machine, computer scanning, digital photography, e-mail, personal Web site and fax,
is illegal. Failure to abide by federal copyright laws may result in litigation and fines.

ISBN: 1-59635-000-8   All rights reserved   Printed in USA   1 2 3 4 5 6 7 8 9